Confident Voices

CORWIN CONNECTED EDUCATORS SERIES

Confident Voices

Digital Tools for Language Acquisition

John Spencer

FOR INFORMATION:

Corwin

A SAGE Company

2455 Teller Road

Thousand Oaks, California 91320

(800) 233-9936

www.corwin.com

SAGE Publications Ltd.

1 Oliver's Yard

55 City Road

London EC1Y 1SP

United Kingdom

SAGE Publications India Pvt. Ltd.

B 1/I 1 Mohan Cooperative Industrial Area

Mathura Road, New Delhi 110 044

India

SAGE Publications Asia-Pacific Pte. Ltd.

3 Church Street

#10-04 Samsung Hub

Singapore 049483

Copyright © 2016 by Corwin

Library of Congress Cataloging-in-Publication Data

Names: Spencer, John (Middle school teacher), author.

Title: Confident voices: digital tools for language acquisition / John Spencer.

Description: Thousand Oaks, California : Corwin, a SAGE Company, 2016. | Series: Corwin connected educators series

Identifiers: LCCN 2015034878 | ISBN 978-1-5063-2302-2 (pbk.: alk. paper)

Subjects: LCSH: English language—Study and teaching—Foreign speakers. | English language—Study and teaching—Technological innovations. | English language—Grammar—Study and teaching. | Educational technology.

Classification: LCC PE1128.A2 S6329 2016 | DDC 428.0078/5—dc23 LC record available at http://lccn.loc.gov/2015034878

This book is printed on acid-free paper.

Acquisitions Editor: Ariel Bartlett

Editorial Assistant: Andrew Olson

Production Editor: Amy Schroller

Copy Editor: Catherine Forrest

Typesetter: C&M Digitals (P) Ltd.

Proofreader: Carole Quandt

Cover and Interior Designer: Janet Kiesel

Marketing Manager: Stephanie Trkay

Certified Chain of Custody

Promoting Sustainable Forestry

www.sfiprogram.org

SFI-01268

SFI label applies to text stock

16 17 18 19 20 10 9 8 7 6 5 4 3 2 1

Contents

Preface

My best friend is a high school math teacher. When I started working on the Corwin Connected Educators series, I excitedly told her about the power of using social media to connect with other educators. I passed on what I learned from the authors in this series: that the greatest resource educators have is each other. At a conference, she heard Jennie Magiera speak and finally made the leap to getting on Twitter. Although I wasn't sure she would continue tweeting, she did, and even joined Twitter chats like #connectedtl and #slowmathchat. A few days later, she texted me saying, "I seriously cannot thank you enough. You have changed my life."

Being "connected" seems deceptively simple: Just get on Twitter, right? But that's really not enough. For those who truly embrace connectedness, it's a lifestyle change, an openness to sharing and learning in an entirely new environment. We're seeing the impact of this shift in mindset worldwide. Policies are changing, new jobs in education are being created, hitherto impossible collaborations are happening, pedagogy is evolving, and there's a heightened awareness of each person's individual impact. All of these changes are explored in the Connected Educators series.

While you can see the full list of books on the series page, we're introducing several new books to the series; they will be published in the fall of 2015 and spring of 2016. These books each contribute something unique and necessary not only for educators who are new to the world of connected education, but also for those who have been immersed in it for some time.

Tom Whitby, coauthor of *The Relevant Educator*, has brought together a group of experienced connected educators in his new book, *The Educator's Guide to Creating Connections*. Contributors Pam Moran, George Couros, Kyle Pace, Adam Bellow, Lisa Nielsen, Kristen Swanson, Steven Anderson, and Shannon McClintock Miller discuss the ways that connectedness has impacted them and the benefits it can have for all educators—policy makers, school and district leaders, and teachers.

While all connected educators are evangelists for being connected, connectedness does not necessarily prevent common problems, such as isolation in leadership. In *Breaking Out of Isolation*, Spike Cook, Jessica Johnson, and Theresa Stager explain how connectedness can alleviate the loneliness leaders can feel in their position and also, when used effectively, help leaders maintain balance in their lives and stay motivated.

For districts and schools embracing the connected mindset and empowering all of their learners to use technology, a solid plan for digital citizenship is a must. In *Digital Citizenship*, Susan Bearden provides a look at how leaders can prepare teachers and students for the new responsibilities of using technology and interacting with others on a truly global platform.

Connected education provides unique opportunities for teachers in their classrooms as well. In *Standing in the Gap*, Lisa Dabbs and Nicol R. Howard explore the ways that social media can specifically help new teachers find resources, connect to mentors, and encourage each other in their careers. Erin Klein, Tom Murray, A. J. Juliani, and Ben Gilpin show how teachers can purposefully integrate technology and empower their students in both physical and digital classrooms in *Redesigning Learning Spaces*.

One of the most powerful impacts connected education can have is in reaching marginalized populations. In *Confident Voices*, John Spencer shows how social media and other technology tools can empower English language learners. Billy Krakower and Sharon LePage Plante have also discovered that technology can reach special and gifted learners as well.

The books in the Corwin Connected Educators series are supported by a companion website featuring videos, articles, downloadable forms, and other resources to help you as you start and continue your journey. Best of all, the authors in the series want to connect with *you!* We've provided their Twitter handles and other contact information on the companion website.

Once you've taken the step to joining a network, don't stop there. Share what you're doing; you never know when it will help someone else!

—*Peter DeWitt, Series Editor*
@PeterMDeWitt

—*Ariel Bartlett, Acquisitions Editor*
@arielkbartlett

About the Author

 **John Spencer** is an assistant professor of instructional technology at George Fox University, where he is focusing on the integration of creative and connective technology with quality pedagogy. He has more than a decade's experience teaching middle school, including a year where he co-led the Twenty-First Century Classrooms, an innovative, STEM-centered, one-to-one initiative with twelve ELL classrooms. He is a frequent keynote speaker and workshop presenter. This last year he delivered a speech at the White House Future Ready Conference. He blogs regularly at SpencerIdeas.org and his work has been featured in *Kappan Magazine, Education Week, The Answer Sheet, Edutopia,* and *Think Inclusive.*

Introduction

A few years ago, I transferred into a self-contained ELL classroom. Suddenly, I had to teach a four-hour language block (an hour of grammar, an hour of reading, an hour of writing, and an hour of oral language development) while also teaching the social studies, math, and science. Having previously taught a project-based gifted inclusion class, I wasn't sure what type of framework I should use in the upcoming school year.

I contacted Jeremy Macdonald, a current technology director, who, at the time, was an expert ELL teacher.

"Could you talk to me about how I should approach ELL?"

"Are you looking for specific language strategies?" he asked.

"I feel like I know about the language support strategies. What I don't know is how to organize a typical lesson."

"What are some of the projects you've done in the past?" he asked.

I explained the Create a Product Project, where they went through the design thinking cycle. I mentioned the Scratch Video Game project and how we blended that with our Cardboard Arcade. I shared my experiences with having students create blogs, podcasts, and videos.

At one point, I sighed and said, "I just wish I could do some of that stuff with this ELL classroom."

"You will," he answered.

"But I have this four hour block and I have students who struggle with English and . . ."

"The lack of language isn't a lack of critical thinking. Your new students deserve the same kind of creative thinking that your current students get to experience," he pointed out. "You just need to build bridges to help them access the language along the way."

Jeremy was right. My ELL students deserved to have a project-based framework. They deserved the same design thinking process. The same choice, inquiry, and creativity that thrived in a gifted class would eventually thrive in a self-contained ELL classroom as well.

At the same time, I had to accommodate for specific language needs. This meant providing more scaffolding for students to access the language that could lead to deeper conversations and higher-level thinking. Although they blogged and created videos and worked on amazing projects, students were using sentence stems, tutorials, extra visuals, and verb tense formulas. This was possible due to the integration of connective and creative digital platforms.

THE POWER OF DIGITAL TOOLS

Language acquisition is often an overlooked area of technology integration. I noticed this recently when I attended an educational technology conference. In session after session, the presenters assumed an automatic level of language mastery among students. The strategies rarely addressed language issues and none of the student examples included an ELL student. I don't blame the presenters. It was a symptom of a larger issue in the educational technology community. There's an assumption that students are already native speakers. There's a sense of normalcy—a linguistic white noise—that permeates these spaces. It isn't an intentional exclusion so much as a systemic, thoughtless lack of inclusion.

This lack of inclusion has had lasting consequences on ELL classrooms. I noticed this when I was an instructional technology coach who specialized in ELL classrooms. Often, ELL teachers struggled to integrate digital tools into their instruction. At times, it was due to a lack of language support. Because the digital platforms rarely address language issues, students lacked the structures to access the language. So, a teacher would learn about blogging and suddenly a student sat in front of an open blog unable to craft a post. Other times, ELL students use digital tools specifically designed for learning a second language. Unfortunately, most of these "personalized" tools are merely adaptive digital worksheets. Students move through the system without getting the chance to be creative, critical thinkers.

This is creating a new digital divide, where ELL students face a digital chasm based not upon access to tools but upon access to language and experiences. This chasm widens with policies and pedagogy that prevent students from experiencing the same creativity and global connections that native speakers experience in project-based classrooms.

It doesn't have to be this way. ELL students can thrive in project-based classrooms through the intentional, thoughtful integration of digital tools. Coupled with the research-based language acquisition strategies, digital tools can empower students to connect with the world. The end result is that students grow in language while also growing as creative thinkers and analytical problem-solvers.

Grammar

People cringe when I tell them I teach grammar. I can see it in their faces. The term conjures up images of a teacher by a chalkboard diagramming sentences while students in rows fill out worksheets on gerunds and participles. Grammar seems to fit into the category of "crap I had to do in school even though it wasn't relevant to my world." I used to mock grammar. I viewed it as archaic and boring—that is, until I had a moment when I saw it as vital to life.

We were doing a social studies project at the time. My students were partnering with other students around the nation to analyze a social issue, comparing and contrasting the causes and effects in each context. It was everything I believed in as a teacher: inquiry-driven, project-based, connective, authentic. But it was also tanking. Students were confused by the texts they were supposed to be analyzing. They were frustrated when their global partners seemed to "get" the language while they struggled.

At first, I assumed the issue was vocabulary. I defined the terms and we practiced using both the content-specific and the academic vocabulary. It didn't work. We moved on to close reading strategies. Again, it failed. Finally, a student said, "I just don't get the sentences."

"Which words?" I asked.

"It's not the words," a student pointed out. "It's the sentences. See this right here 'had been watching.' What does that mean?"

Another student pointed out a sentence with passive voice. Still another, showed me a sentence written in the future perfect progressive verb tense. To be honest, I didn't know anything about the actual verb tenses. Being a native English speaker from a place of educational privilege, these sentence structures were normal to me.

> Suddenly grammar went from a meaningless drill to a vital part of accessing information in a connected world.

It was in this moment that I realized the chasm created when students could not access the verb tense. Suddenly grammar went from a meaningless drill to a vital part of accessing information in a connected world. Over the next few years, I grew to love grammar and, in the process, I came to terms with common cultural myths about grammar.

MYTH #1: GRAMMAR ISN'T RELEVANT ANYMORE

Initially, I placed grammar in the same category as slide rules and library cards. I figured it was like penmanship practice—nice and proper but not particularly relevant. After all, I used the grammar check when I writing and I relied on the green squiggly line to tell me when I screwed up. Now I see grammar as a necessary component to understanding information.

MYTH #2: WE UNDERSTAND GRAMMAR BY SHEER IMMERSION

I failed to notice that the authors who created and published information often used complex grammar. English Language Learners often struggle with complex grammatical structures because they are the structures used in writing but rarely used in conversational speech. Native speakers (especially those who come from a print-rich background) have more exposure to reading and listening to language with complex grammatical structures. Thus a sentence with a complex verb tense feels normal to a native speaker while feeling overwhelming to someone still learning a second language.

MYTH #3: GRAMMAR IS ALL ABOUT RULES

Growing up, there was always a certain "gotcha" element to grammar. It was all about avoiding mistakes rather than accessing language. I learned not to split infinitives (not actually a violation of correct grammar) or end sentences with a preposition (also not a true violation of correct grammar). What I missed was that grammar is less about rules and more about a system of language. It's what allows our words to make sense. I've learned to focus less on correcting what is wrong and more on seeing grammar as a way to open new doors to language. Grammar should be expansive rather than limiting; descriptive rather than prescriptive.

MYTH #4: GRAMMAR IS BORING

I used to think that grammar was boring. I knew people who could debate the Oxford comma for hours. My experience with grammar had been fill-in-the-blank workbooks and hours spent diagramming sentences. Now I realize that grammar can be fun, exciting, relevant, and integrated into other subject areas.

This was a slow evolution for me. I initially presented verb tense formulas to students and told them, "This is going to be a little boring but it will ultimately help you with other subjects that are more fun."

However, as I saw the direct connection between grammar and choice-driven student writing, I realized that grammar could be fun. I started adding visual elements and examples that piqued student interest. Over time, I realized that certain verb tenses complemented the essential questions we were forming for blogs and podcasts.

MYTH #5: GRAMMAR IS SCARY

I've known many first language adults who are terrified of grammar. Many adults have been shamed for a simple verb-subject agreement error, often by people online who delight in a stiff fixation in being grammatically correct. After all, people use self-described phrases like "Grammar Nazi," that, beyond being culturally insensitive, also imply an overbearing, rigid, and harsh approach to grammar. It's a no-win situation. We are expected to remain grammatically correct at all times, with the fear of a punishment and no promise of a reward. We don't exactly compliment one another's command of grammar. Nobody says, "Hey Dave, you nailed those clauses in the meeting today. That gerund was amazing and your command of the future perfect verb tense was dazzling."

Indeed, a quick scan of the last sentence suggests that grammar is more difficult than rocket science (which might be true; I've never attempted rocket science). The vocabulary alone can feel overwhelming.

It is no wonder, then, that second language learners arrive to school terrified by grammar. It feels like a daunting subject to master and they have to do this in a social context that implies that mistakes are not to be tolerated.

MYTH #6: GRAMMAR CAN'T BE PERSONALIZED

As a student, I hated grammar work because we spent so long practicing things that I already knew. Any child of the eighties could tell you what an adverb was. We'd been using them with *Mad Libs*. In addition, we had no choice in what we were constructing. We never had the chance to explore how grammar connected to anything personal. Thus our grammar work never included choice, relevance, or creativity. We didn't get the chance to practice at our own pace. It was a one-size-fits-all, drill-and-kill framework that fed into the lie that grammar was boring and irrelevant.

A DIFFERENT APPROACH

When I first realized that students needed grammar, I stopped the projects and gave short mini-lessons on verb tenses, clauses, and transitional words. By default, I taught grammar in the same way that I had learned it. Slowly, though, I began to shift my paradigm:

- From isolated practice to an integrated part of reading, writing, and speaking
- From standardized instruction to personalized learning
- From focusing on rules to seeing grammar as a system (and thus including both the "how" and the "why")
- From rigid to flexible (with a heavy emphasis on student choice)
- From paper and pencil to integrated technology
- From independent work to interdependent work

Over time, I started to approach grammar differently. I embraced creativity and student choice. I integrated grammar into the other subjects. I realized that students needed not only grammar skills but also a conceptual understanding of the function of language.

GRAMMAR-BASED BLOGGING

Grammar can work well as a starting point for a writer's workshop. It begins with a verb-tense study that then transitions into a listening and speaking activity before finally leading to choice-driven writing.

I start it with a series of high-interest provocative questions. I add the questions as an overlay over a Creative Commons visual. For example, if I want students to use the future perfect verb tense, I might use the following questions in a slideshow:

- What will you have accomplished by the age of twenty-three?
- What will we have invented as a society by the year 2037?
- Are we going to have perfected magnetic travel before we have perfected flying cars?
- Will you have finished college before starting your full-time career?
- What is one of your goals? What challenges will you have faced before accomplishing this goal?
- What are some of the things you are going to have completed before you finish high school?

This verb tense is tricky, so I break students up into small groups and have them discuss when the perfect tense is being used. Is it referring to something in the past, present, or future? What parts make sense? What parts are tricky? After doing a pair-share, we talk about the purpose and context of the perfect tense.

Next, I have students go to a blog post with the verb tense. I include the fact that "going to" is often used casually in the perfect tense. We practice the verb tense verbally by looking at a picture and creating a bank of nouns (broken into objects and direct objects) and verbs that are then placed into the verb tense formula. We also practice with the declarative, interrogative, and negative sentence structures through doing a question-and-answer conversation connected to the original visual. At this time, students who are using the verb tense correctly can add adjectives and adverbs to their sentences.

After practicing this through listening and speaking, students move on to writing. Here, they choose from one of the visual writing ideas and insert the picture into a blog post. They highlight and copy the verb tense formula and use it as a basis of a declarative thesis statement. From here, they add additional supporting details while still keeping the post in the same verb tense.

Students who are still struggling with the verb tense get a chance to practice it through choice-based writing. This repetition helps solidify the verb tense while still allowing for students to engage in a high-interest activity that connects to a critical thinking question. Students who have mastered the verb tense are encouraged to improve their writing by adding multiple clauses, using transitional phrases, including additional details, and incorporating adverbs and adjectives.

The next day, students leave comments on one another's posts. I include optional sentence stems that use the verb tense formula. I don't require students to use the same verb tense in the comment. Instead, I treat this as a formative assessment to see if students are comfortable enough with the verb tense to use it in a blog comment.

GRAMMAR PODCASTS

As students grow comfortable with verb tenses, they can create thematic podcasts and publish them to the world. For example, the conditional verb form can be tricky for some students. They struggle with when to use would, should, or could. They have a hard time figuring out how to modify the verbs. After speaking and blogging with the conditional form, they begin a short podcast project on the theme of possibilities. Beginning with the stem, "What would happen if _____?" they work in teams with doing research online. As students seek out accurate information, they are faced with the natural context of the conditional form. So, each step, from the question to the informational reading to the paraphrasing afterward, reinforces the conditional form. Students take the paraphrased information and turn it into a list-styled blog

post with the stem "Seven Things That Could/Might Happen If
_____." Next, students develop a set of questions and an initial
introduction script for their podcast. After rehearsing it a few
times, they record a podcast.

If you're interested in going more global, students can interview an
expert on the topic and include it in the final podcast. They can
use email, direct messaging, social media, or video conferencing
(which would allow students to include the interview in the final
podcast). To extend it even further globally, your ELL students
could partner with students throughout the world—especially if
the global students are still learning English as well. Using shared
documents or spreadsheets, they can keep their facts in a central
location, edit a shared document for the script, and video record
the podcast using video conferencing software (such as a Google
Hangouts or Skype).

There are some things to consider before starting a grammar podcast. It's important here that the verb tense fits the topic of the
podcast. For example, a history-related podcast would work well
with the simple past, past progressive, or past perfect verb tenses.
In addition, it's critical to be realistic about the difficulties of syn-
chronous communications when choosing a global partner. Time
zones can be an issue when trying to do video conferencing.
Technology and policies can vary from school to school. Finally,
this type of project works best when a teacher is already a connected educator and therefore has developed relationships with
teachers around the world.

ENDLESS POSSIBILITIES

Grammar is the initial bridge that makes the English language
possible for ELL students. Instead of being a boring activity or a
strict set of rules, grammar is actually the structure from which
language grows. It is expansive rather than limiting. While I initially assumed grammar would be something irrelevant or boring,
I now see that it can be exciting and meaningful when it begins
with an authentic, tech-integrated framework.

Next Steps

- Take some time to explore all the verb tenses in the English language. If you find that boring, look up all the Estonian verb tenses for fun.

- See if there are any connections between grammar rules in English and in a common second language. Most of my second language learners spoke Spanish. I was able to show similarities between the progressive verb tenses in both languages.

- Try using a chart with a specific grammar verb tense on one column, a tech-integrated task in the middle, and additional language supports on the far right.

Verb Tense	Tech-Integrated Task	Additional Language Supports
Future perfect	Podcast on what the future will be like, answering the question, "What will we have invented by 2045?"	Question and answer stems modeling the declarative, interrogative and negative sentence types
Future progressive	Blog post answering the question, "What will you be doing after you graduate college?"	A paragraph cloze for students who need it and a bank of work-related, school-related, and life-related nouns and verbs
Past perfect progressive	A video interview using the past perfect verb tense to ask whether people had or had not been doing certain things on a specific day	Question and answer stems, varying from simple to complex

- Students often need to access grammar help when reading a word problem in math or a history textbook. You might want to create a digital space where students can access verb tense formulas, along with tutorials. I've found that short videos and .gifs can be helpful.

- Make a list of great authentic teaching strategies (student choice, inquiry, and so on). Find ways to incorporate those into grammar lessons.

●●● FOR REFLECTION ●●●

1. What are some ways you can push a growth mindset in grammar? How can you help students know that mistakes are a part of the process? What analogies could you use (like riding a bike)?

2. What are some ways you can keep grammar from being boring?

3. Would it help to avoid the term "grammar"? Would a different term help to avoid the negative connotations?

4. What strategies can you use to help students see grammar as a discovery of how language works rather than a list of rules?

CHAPTER 2

Vocabulary

I thought I had nailed the lesson plan. Students were preparing for debate-styled podcasts by reading an assortment of high-interest informational texts. I had paid close attention to reading levels and allowed students to choose which texts they wanted to read. On the surface, the lesson was a success.

However, I knew it wasn't working when I noticed five different students who were completely checked out. One student drew a complex stick figure ninja battle. Another student stared at the wall and two others sat there talking about soccer.

I approached the stick figure ninja artist and asked, "Why aren't you doing your work? Is the topic boring?"

He shook his head. "I just don't get it."

"Tell me what you don't understand," I said.

"All of it," he mumbled.

"What do you mean all of it?" I asked.

"I mean all of it," he growled.

"Okay, but what part is confusing you the most?"

"The words. They don't make sense," he pointed out.

"We went over vocabulary." I pointed to the wall with every content vocabulary word. I reminded him that we had already defined the words, along with a definition, sample sentence, and TPR (total physical response).

"I know the social studies words," he said. "I just don't get the rest of it."

I had a similar conversation with two other students in that same class period. Each of these students spoke English at a functional level but had a difficult time accessing academic texts. It was at that point that I realized that many of my ELL students were struggling to access the text because they lacked the academic language needed to wrestle with the concepts.

I also realized that many of these students had internalized the myth that they weren't smart enough to understand higher-level concepts because they had never felt empowered to speak the language at a higher level. They felt lost, not only when reading academic texts, but also when participating in a discussion about a specific concept or idea.

It was at this point that I realized the value of explicit Tier Two vocabulary instruction. Most of my ELL students were proficient in the conversational Tier One vocabulary. Like the rest of my students, I had taught the low-frequency, content-specific Tier Three vocabulary. However, they struggled with the Tier Two vocabulary found across all content areas. So, what felt like second nature to many of the native speakers became a chasm for my ELL students. However, with the help of technology, I began building bridges so that students could cross the chasm.

THE POWER OF SOCIAL CURATION

When I first began focusing on vocabulary, I used a passive approach to front-loading. Here, I would pick out five or six high-frequency Tier Two vocabulary words and write them on the board. I would then define the words and have students repeat the definition in a choral format after me. Unfortunately, it became an exercise in compliance rather than a chance to unlock difficult vocabulary. This process failed to respect student agency.

Things began to change when I asked students to find pictures that demonstrated the idea of a Tier Two vocabulary word. The pictures could be more literal or more metaphorical. Students would find the picture and add it to their vocabulary blogs. Afterward, they would define the academic word in their own words (based upon the definition I gave) and use it in a sample sentence. As a class, we would define other words in the word family. Students would then use the label function to find synonyms. Using the category function on the blog, they chose specific content areas where the words might be used. For many students, this was an opportunity to realize that academic words had multiple meanings across various content areas.

While this process meant we uncovered words at a slower pace, it also meant that the words stuck with the students. Reviewing a word (including a word in the word family) was as simple as using the search function in the vocabulary blogs.

Furthermore, this process allowed students to build their own vocabulary by curating the words. Here, students were deciding how to organize the language. The tagging system allowed each student to find connections and relationships between words. Students felt empowered to define the language in a way that made sense to them. Over time, students began using their vocabulary blogs without being prompted. This was eye-opening for me as a teacher when I noticed students began adding words that I had assumed they knew or omitting words I assumed they didn't know.

The process grew more social as students discovered the "reblog" function. Suddenly, students were not only curating the language but also curating the vocabulary posts of other students. They began leaving comments on one another's posts, asking questions about words and getting into discussions about when a particular word would be used instead of another word. These moments were rare. I wish I had encouraged more social curating from the beginning. However, it was a lesson for me in how social curation could empower students to own the process.

To a native speaker, a vocabulary blog might seem bizarre. However, for my ELL students, the vocabulary blogs became a chance to geek out about language. It became a chance for students to build their own bridge on a journey to make sense out of academic concepts.

VOCABULARY CONCEPT MAPS

The term *vocabulary words* often conjures up images of lists with definitions. We grow up seeing words in lists on handouts and vocabulary quizzes. Even dictionaries follow a linear format. However, words are not linear. They do not exist sequentially in an isolated format. Rather, every word is a connection to another word in an ongoing semantic web of ideas. When students make sense out of these connections, they have a deeper, richer understanding of the words.

While this is a built-in aspect of the vocabulary blogs, sometimes it helps to have students create their own linguistic concept maps. I typically start this process offline with printed cards, soda cans, and yarn. Here, small groups of students take yarn and wrap it around a soda can with a particular academic word on it. Next, they send the yarn across the room to another word with a similar meaning. I provide sentence stems so that students can discuss why a particular word connects to another word.

After doing a visual-spatial semantic web, students move to creating vocabulary concept maps using an online mind-mapping program. Students color-code words and connections as they compare and contrast words. In some cases, students change the shapes to represent morphology into the different parts of speech.

Next, students take a snapshot of their concept maps and describe one pathway of how a word might relate to other words. This can be done verbally in a pair-share or by using the record function on a smartphone. Initially, the teacher might need to give an example and a sample sentence stem such as "_____ is similar to _____ because they both mean _____. However,_____ tends to mean _____ while _____ means _____." The goal here is for students to discuss similarities and difference in words while also analyzing the connotation and ideal contexts of using specific words.

In the process, it becomes both an opportunity to build connections between words while also acting as an alternative assessment method. While traditional vocabulary tests measure whether or not a student recognizes a word, linguistic concept maps assess what connections a student can make between various academic words. Instead of finding out what students *don't* know, it is a chance to see what students are learning in a connective, visual way.

While the initial assignment can be time-consuming, students can continue to add additional Tier Two vocabulary to their concept maps throughout the year. It becomes an ongoing visual representation of both the language they are acquiring and the connections they are making.

ANNOTATING TEXT

ELL students often need additional vocabulary scaffolding in the midst of reading a passage. One helpful strategy is to have students annotate the vocabulary within a text using either an online annotation application or a shared document. This allows students to use context clues to define words while also encouraging them to define academic language that they find confusing. The teacher can also add notes and links to resources, such as prefix and suffix lists.

Although it is helpful to model digital annotation with students, it is also critical that the process remain flexible. If students see annotation as a lockstep procedure that they have to follow, they are more likely to focus on the strategy and less likely to focus on the words they are trying to learn. Other times, they end up annotating a document out of compliance rather than seeing it as a bridge to access the language.

For this reason, I mention the various annotation tools that students can use and ask them to choose ones that work for them. Some students use highlighters with color codes to match the parts of speech. Others highlight words and link them to the words in their vocabulary blogs. Some students highlight words and leave a rollover comment with a synonym. Some students break the phrases up and add synonyms in parentheses using a different text color. The key here is that they feel empowered to make sense out of the words as they read.

Due to the inherently social nature of digital tools, students can also collaborate on text annotation. In these situations, I team students up into groups of four and have each student leave comments on words they find confusing. Some of the conversations happen verbally, as students discuss the meaning of a particular word or phrase. Often, though, the conversations happen on the margins of the text. In these moments, the entire class feels empowered to share their vocabulary knowledge while also feeling the permission to be open about what they don't understand.

CONCLUSION

ELL students need to feel empowered to make sense out of the language on their own terms and in their own ways. This can mean creating their own content on a vocabulary blog, adding connections on a concept mapping program, or annotating a text on a shared document. While many of these strategies can be done with paper and pencil, digital tools allow students to play around with the language in a space that is both more social and more flexible. In the process, they grow more confident in their abilities and more competent in their comprehension.

Next Steps

- Create a word bank of the most frequent and most difficult Tier Two vocabulary words. Turn the word bank into a pre-assessment, asking students to define each word. Use this as a starting point for the rest of your vocabulary word work.

- Choose one of the strategies listed above and test it out with a classroom. It might help to start with a technology tool you are already using (like a Google Document).

- Create a brainstorm of ways you can make vocabulary acquisition more collaborative, such as a shared vocabulary blog.

- Keep in mind that many of these strategies take a lot of time at first but eventually they become efficient.

- See if you can find cognates between a student's native language and an academic word in English. For example, given its Latin roots, *differentiate* is similar to *diferenciar* in Spanish and *differencier* in French.

 FOR REFLECTION

1. Why is it important for students to create their own definitions of vocabulary words?

2. How can you help students understand the connections between words?

3. What are the biggest vocabulary challenges that your second language learners face? What are you currently doing to meet these challenges?

4. What are some ways that technology can improve vocabulary acquisition?

CHAPTER 3

Oral Language

As a Technology Specialist for Language Acquisition (a much longer title than simply "teacher"), I got the chance to work with an amazing sixth grade ELL teacher named Miriam Combs.

On one afternoon, I walked around the classroom listening to students discussing problem-solving and real-world contexts. After searching out scenarios, they were working with partners to develop their own math problems.

"I'm not sure if that's really a linear relationship, because the variable isn't constant," a girl points out.

"Why do you think it isn't linear?" her partner asks.

"It won't go on forever. You only have so many options," she says, pointing to the cable television package options.

I walked past another group where a boy said, "You came up with a realistic linear relationship but I'm wondering if you included taxes. Would that change the answer?"

As they shifted from setting up to solving the problems, students compared and contrasted mathematical processes.

"Is there a more efficient way to solve this equation?" a student asked.

"There might be, but I wanted to use something I know would work for every linear equation," his partner answered.

"I would have solved it by isolating the variable first," the student shot back.

There were moments when the debates got intense. A few times, students felt frustrated by their own mistakes. However, the discussions were deep in thought and rich in academic language. Students were analyzing mathematical systems and processes while also building their conceptual knowledge of the properties of numbers.

This moment was amazing. However, it didn't start out that way. Students began the year struggling with oral language development. They had a hard time listening to academic language and they struggled to engage in academic discourse. For some, it was an issue of grammatical complexity. For others, it was a matter of higher-level, Tier Two vocabulary. Still, for other students, it was a matter of pace. If someone spoke too quickly, they felt lost and they disengaged out of frustration.

Inevitably, though, students grew in their oral language development because of the frequency and structure of academic discourse. It began with scaffolding. Miriam modeled the thinking process by using sentence, question, and paragraph stems that she posted around the room. They practiced together before recording their conversations on their devices and using an online form as a self-reflection rubric. Over time, she added simpler sentence stems (housed online) with more flexibility and fewer words. Students customized the language and chose which stems worked best for them. Eventually, they moved away from the scaffolding and began creating their own academically rich phrases.

This is one of the many tech-integrated ways that teachers can leverage technology for oral language development.

DIGITAL STUDENT-TEACHER CONFERENCING

When I first taught ELL, I noticed that students seemed to improve in their oral language development after a five-minute conference with me. While it was important for them to use academic language with one another, the one-to-one conversation with a teacher made a huge difference. It also became a bold reminder that listening to me deliver direct instruction wasn't very helpful. The sheer number of times a student would ask me to repeat myself helped me to see that they were not necessarily tracking with typical direct instruction. Moreover, the chance for students to ask questions and push a dialogue helped me to see that oral language required constant interaction. Simply put, students had not been given enough of an opportunity to engage in an academic conversation with teachers.

It was at this point that I realized the power of voice commenting systems. Here, I could leave a comment with academic language (through a system like Voice Thread) and students could listen to the comment multiple times. In some cases, they could slow down or speed up the comment as well. It became a personalized method of listening to academic language in a way that directly connected to their work. But it was also a chance for students to think about how they would respond and then formulate their own verbal comment back. Because the sentence stems were available at any time, students could simply pull up another tab in their browser and access instant scaffolding.

Suddenly, I found myself engaging in deeper, richer conversations with students as they analyzed their work. Because of the asynchronous nature of voice threads, students could listen to my feedback as many times as they wanted and they could take their time crafting a response. This helped reduce the affective filter as they grew more confident in their language. In addition, the chance to play their own comments back to me helped students monitor and adjust to their own verbal output. They began self-adjusting when they heard their own mistakes.

These digital conferences had a few added bonuses that I had never considered. First, students had to rely solely on the oral language. They could not rely on nonverbal cues to make sense out of academic language. In addition, students could listen to former voice threads and hear, firsthand, how they had improved in speaking. Finally, they were not limited by the space and time constraints of traditional face-to-face conferences.

THE POWER OF MULTIMEDIA CONTENT CREATION

A few years back, my principal asked me to run the morning announcements. I rounded up a group of five students who rotated between being the anchors, reporters, and writers on our morning news crew. However, two weeks into it, my principal pulled me aside.

"I love the morning announcements. I love the background you made. The whole thing looks polished."

"Thanks," I answered.

"But I noticed that you don't have any ELL students in the mix," he said.

"None of them tried out."

"They won't try out. Most of them are embarrassed of their language level."

I nodded. "So how do I help them become more confident?"

"You get them on the morning announcements. You recruit them. You find something that they are really good at and you tell them that you need their skills."

I took his advice and found two ELL students who were amazing at video editing. At first, they stayed behind the scenes in an editing area. However, I slowly started asking them to practice in our short rehearsals and eventually encouraged them to do some prerecorded videos. Over time, they grew more comfortable and eventually took on the role of news anchors. It was a bold reminder that one of the best ways to help ELL students grow in confidence is to find opportunities for them to create multimedia content.

Student videos are one way that students can leverage multimedia content for oral language development. Here, students can start by crafting a script with the help of grammatical structures or sentence stems. This allows students to feel well prepared and less nervous about the moment of speaking. Next, they create videos connected to their content area. It might be a video "movie preview" of a novel, a short tutorial for a math problem, or a roundtable debate on a social issue. The nice thing here is that students can make mistakes and try again. It becomes a subtle way to push a growth mindset because they know they can always repeat the process and improve. Afterward, students work on editing the finished product by using a video program such as iMovie. As students edit out and re-record parts of the video, they begin to see trends in the oral language development. Here they get to self-assess their language in a way that feels empowering rather than discouraging.

A second, shorter option is an annotated slideshow. Here students create a slideshow (on Keynote or PowerPoint) with text and Creative Commons visuals. After writing a script, they record the audio to go with the slides. Most presentation programs will also allow students to export the slideshow into a short video that they can publish to the world.

The shortest and easiest option is a podcast. With a podcast, students can record with their smart phones and edit using an audio editing program like Audacity or Garage Band. One of the key advantages is that students don't have to worry about props, lighting, or staging. They can read a script or use sentence stems in the moment and the listener never knows about it. I've noticed that many of my ELL students prefer to start with a script that they rehearse and eventually transition into sentence stems or even a basic outline.

In each of these options, students grow in confidence as they publish their multimedia works with the world. I've seen students who were concerned about their accents or worried about their pronunciations and pacing grow into confidant speakers. It becomes a powerful paradigm shift as students, once self-conscious about their accents or worried about their language level, begin to speak confidently and share their insights with the world.

It's also an opportunity for students to self-reflect on their progress. When students edit their video or audio, they get a chance to pick up on some of the mistakes they might be missing in the moment. Instead of relying on external assessments, they get the chance to self-reflect and think through specific steps they need to make to continue improving in oral language development.

CONCLUSION

Oral language development can be difficult for ELL students. Often the traditional structure of school means students encounter longer lectures spoken at a pace that makes comprehension difficult. However, when students are given the chance to speak with one another and to find their own voice, they grow in their oral language development. Digital tools amplify this by allowing students to record, listen, slow down, and edit audio. In the process, they become confident speakers ready to share their voices with the world.

Next Steps

- Develop sentence stems for the most common areas of academic discourse, including: compare and contrast, making sense out of meaning, learning reflections, analyzing a text, and comparing processes.

- Start with digital recording tools that are quick and intuitive for students. While there is a time and place for audio editing, simple tools can be a powerful way for students to capture their voices and listen to trends.

- Pay close attention to the affective filter of English Language Learners. Many students will be nervous and scared about speaking, so a positive classroom culture will be critical for student success.

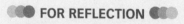

FOR REFLECTION

1. Why is oral language development important for other areas of language acquisition?

2. How can digital audio tools help students improve in their oral language development?

3. What are the biggest psychological and emotional barriers that students face in oral language development? How can you empower students to feel more confident about their voices?

4. What are some strategies you can use to help students use complex academic discourse throughout the school day?

Writing

Ten years ago, when I first encouraged students to pursue digital writing, I treated blogging like a digital notebook. The results were underwhelming. Students walked in each day and completed a prompt I had written on the board. We had such creative post titles as "Bell Work—January 11th" or "Lab Report—February 3rd." These were essentially online versions of what I had required in the physical notebooks. The blogs had no comments or pictures or even much of a student voice. After all, my students had no real concept of writing for an authentic audience. It was simply an easier way for me to do binder checks.

Things began to change when a student asked me as simple question.

"Do you ever blog?"

"Yeah, three or four times a week," I answered.

"For fun?"

I nodded.

"What do you blog about?"

"I blog about my kids or about school. I guess I like to write about creative stuff, too."

"Do you read other people's blogs?"

I nodded.

"Really? You read those for fun?"

"Yeah, I read blogs about history and books and graphic design, but I also read a lot of teacher blogs."

She shook her head and turned back to her computer. I looked at her screen and noticed the contrast between the blogs that I read and the blog post she was writing. The blogs I read began with ideas rather than prompts. People wrote things they were passionate about. They told stories. They wrote how-to posts. They geeked out about things that piqued their curiosity. Often, they added a layer of multimedia. Most posts I read had at least one picture, along with a catchy title to grab the reader's attention.

But here's the thing. I had never once read a personal or professional blog with a post title like "Bell Work—November 12th." Never once. So at that point, I shifted my approach. I realized that the real power of a blog was in the potential for students to share their thoughts with the world based upon their own interests. So, a kid who loved all things culinary could write a foodie blog. A student who was passionate about sports could write a sports blog.

Over the next ten years, I shifted even further into student choice and voice in blogging. As social media grew, I had students share their published work with the world. As students began publishing globally, their confidence increased. They realized that there was an authentic audience interested in

> I realized that the real power of a blog was in the potential for students to share their thoughts with the world based upon their own interests.

their thoughts. Suddenly they were expert authors with something valuable to publish rather than being the lowest subgroup score on a standardized writing test.

Ten Tips for Starting Student Blogging

Each year, I have students fill out a survey of which digital platforms they have used. On average, less than 10 percent of all students have read a blog post and less than 5 percent have ever written a blog post. It is no surprise, then, when they initially use a blog as a digital notebook. So here are ten tips for getting started on student blogging:

1. Help students find blogs that fit their interests. It's hard for students to know what to write in a blog post if they have never had the chance to read blogs.

2. Ask students to write with the goal of getting readers hooked. I explain the importance of catchy titles, an active voice (with personality) and thought-provoking content.

3. Structure time for students to read one another's posts. Encourage students to comment on the content rather than the style of writing. In the same way, as a teacher, you should avoid leaving style comments on student posts and instead use the comments as a chance to model respectful dialogue.

4. Integrate multimedia into the blog posts. This could be a photo, a video, an audio snippet, or a slideshow.

5. Define the audience of a blog post. If it's a personal post, help students learn to publish it privately. If it's a global audience, ask students to find places where they can share to an audience that would actually want to read the post. One option is to partner with other teachers so that students are connected with someone from a different geographic location.

6. Embrace student choice. While there is certainly a time and a place for teacher-directed writing assignments, bloggers

(Continued)

(Continued)

generally have more autonomy. They write about the topics they care about. The same should be true of student bloggers.

7. Teach students about copyright. This includes avoiding plagiarism in writing and making sure they have permission to use visuals or multimedia. I usually include a specific lesson on Creative Commons for that reason.

8. Find ways that students can assess their own work. This includes checklists, rubrics, and self-reflection questions. The better they are at self-assessment the more confident they grow as writers and the more aware they are in where they need to improve.

9. Communicate with parents. Blogs can seem different and even scary for parents. Make sure to communicate the privacy protections you are putting in place to ensure students remain safe while publishing to the world.

10. Support language acquisition in each part of the writing process. Use the same types of student discourse, sentence stems, and vocabulary strategies in student blogging as you would use in other aspects of your instruction.

THE ENTIRE WRITING PROCESS

It is not uncommon for an ELL student to struggle when first introduced to blogging. After all, most blogging platforms were not designed with language acquisition in mind. They offer virtually no language support in the composition or editing of writing. However, this doesn't have to be an insurmountable obstacle. With the right strategies, teachers can support ELL students throughout the entire writing process.

As mentioned previously in the grammar chapter, I have found that verb tense formulas can be a practical starting point for student blogging—especially when the formula connects to a larger driving question. It also helps to include student choice. This is why I use visual writing ideas to spark student interest. Here students look at a writing idea with a question or statement, a photograph, and an audio recording (which we use on Write About). These differ from writing prompts in that prompts are meant to require writing while ideas are meant to inspire writing. The choice element is critical for engagement while the visual element allows students to see a concrete example of a more abstract idea.

Students at a lower language level begin by looking at the picture and generating a list of verbs, nouns, and adjectives (or even adverbs if possible). Next, they use the verb tense formula (or a paragraph stem based upon the verb tense) and begin writing their first post. A teacher can include plenty of Creative Commons photos to help ensure that students still retain choice and agency even when they need extra scaffolding.

Students at a more advanced language level might skip the entire process and begin by selecting a writing idea and pre-writing with a graphic organizer, a set of sentence stems, or an outline. In terms of grammar, advanced students might focus on adding clauses or more complex transitional phrases.

Teachers can provide customized tutorials, such as transition word banks or sample paragraphs, on a website, shared document, or wiki. I've found that students respond well to a combination of text, video, and animated .gifs. This allows for instant access to customized help in both grammar and writing. The multimedia format ensures students are accessing help in multiple modalities.

As they move into the editing phase, students can use annotated documents (such as a Google Document) in a writers' workshop model. Here, the editor (whether a teacher or another student) can leave feedback by highlighting the text and leaving a comment. They can also link to the tutorials, word banks, or graphic organizers that students might need.

As students move from the revision to the editing phase, teachers can use online forms (such as Google Forms) to house self-editing and peer-editing checklists. Teachers can modify the forms to include elements of language acquisition (such as complexity of sentence structure of difficulty of vocabulary) along with using the typical editing elements of word choice, mechanics and sentence fluency. Teachers can check the data from one central location in order to pull small groups or to send additional resources. In addition, students can analyze their own writing data by looking at the word count, words per sentence, or reading level (using an online reading level generator) and setting goals to reach a higher level of text complexity.

Eventually, when students are ready to publish a post, they can add labels along with Creative Commons pictures, embedded videos, or audio to their posts. Teachers can also give students the opportunity to leave comments on one another's blog posts. I use a set of blog comment stems to help guide students in how to comment on the ideas of posts rather than simply saying, "nice job" and "good work."

It doesn't have to end here, though. Teachers can help connect to a global audience by using the #comments4kids hashtag and sending posts out to social media. If the blogging platform has custom groups (such as Write About) students can select themed and topical writing groups. If that isn't possible, teachers can create groups on learning management systems, such as Edmodo, or partner with another class across the world. Long-distance connections thrive in blogging because of the asynchronous communication and the device-agnostic nature of most platforms.

Over the course of the blogging unit, students are able to go through the entire writing process while also growing in their language development. However, because the experience is so personalized, it never feels phony or formulaic.

Digital eBooks are another great way for students to publish to the world. While the functions are similar (text with the ability to embed multimedia) eBooks tend to be closer in format to a traditional book. Readers go through sequential chapters rather than chronological posts. While some eBooks include interactive tools, most eBooks don't include user commenting. The end result tends to be something more polished and formal than a typical blog post.

FULL INTEGRATION

While blogs and eBooks tend to focus on the entire writing process, sometimes it helps to integrate writing into other content areas. When students create podcasts, they also learn how to write efficient informational text in the show notes. When comparing and contrasting mathematical processes, students can take snapshots of their work alongside annotated directions for how to solve a problem. Similarly, as students compose slideshow presentations, they can practice writing in a way that requires very little prewriting or revision.

The goal here is for students to get their thoughts out quickly and efficiently without spending hours on a specific text. For example, students in my class work on a design project where they have to identity a problem that consumers face and create a realistic product solution that people would actually buy. Each part of the design thinking process includes writing—whether it is the initial report of market research, the plan, the description of the prototype, the marketing campaign, or the final website where they present their product.

The end result is that students grow in their writing endurance. Often, it doesn't feel like a writing assignment, because the focus is on the ideas rather than the text itself. However, these moments of practice become opportunities to reinforce the quality writing strategies they are using when they craft blog posts.

Next Steps

- Find a digital publishing platform and treat it as that: a place for students to publish their work in their own style, based upon their own interests. The less it feels like school, the more they will write.

- Develop a set of sentence stems, paragraph stems, and cloze activities for struggling writers. Differentiate these according to language needs.
- Provide tutorials and help texts (i.e., a bank of transition words, a tutorial for writing a paragraph), along with writing-related vocabulary words.

●● FOR REFLECTION ●●

1. Why is student choice important for developing writers?
2. How can you connect writing to grammar? What are some areas where the two can blend together?
3. What are the biggest weaknesses language learners face as they approach writing? What strategies can you use to help students grow in these areas?
4. Why is it important for students to find an authentic audience?

Reading

When I first began teaching ELL, I decided I would "teach it like the gifted class." I would embrace student choice and inquiry. Students would engage in meaningful silent reading before participating in literary circles. If an authentic, choice-driven framework could work for gifted students, why not embrace that framework in an ELL classroom?

Unfortunately, it didn't work out as planned. Students stared at the screen during the student-driven research projects. They wanted to answer difficult questions but they struggled with the basic comprehension of the complex texts they were reading during research. They struggled with the online literary circles I created. While they enjoyed the student choice, they were often limited by language and vocabulary.

I was tempted, at this point, to abandon this approach altogether. Maybe my students needed the basic basal readers. Perhaps I needed to do long, guided practice articles together with the class. However, students began to thrive when I added scaffolding that would support their language acquisition. By focusing on the language acquisition strategies listed in the previous chapters, students were able to grow as more confident, independent readers.

- Vocabulary strategies: Students created vocabulary blogs and concept maps as part of the front-loading and review of vocabulary terms. In the moment, they used online annotation tools to make sense out of difficult texts. Students were also able to make sense out of difficult words when they used the vocabulary context clues and the morphology strategies.

- Grammar practice: As students began to make sense out of difficult verb tenses, they were able to pick apart difficult texts. For the first time ever, students were reading and understanding grade-level texts. They learned how to take apart multiple clauses and phrases.

- Blending reading and writing: Students practiced the reading strategies during the research phases of their writing projects (blogs, eBooks, and websites), often citing evidence to prove a point. However, they also wrote about what they were reading as they engaged in online discussions, literary circles and creative projects.

- Oral language: As they learned to listen and speak complex academic language, students viewed complex texts as a natural extension of higher level thinking. In some cases, the discussions were a part of summarizing and making sense out of the text. In other cases, the discussions required students to cite evidence of facts they had found in the text. However, as they grew in their oral language development, students improved as readers.

In other words, I began blending the scaffolding mentioned in other chapters with our reading lessons. This resulted in an integration of each of the areas of language. As a result, students were able to access the text while also thriving on choice, inquiry, and creativity.

CHOICE AND INQUIRY

At the beginning of the year, I ask students to describe what they think when they heard the words "informational text." Typically, students describe feeling bored and frustrated as a teacher passes out an article for them to read. Students see informational text as the vegetables they have to eat before they get a chance to have the dessert of reading a novel or a story. This mentality isn't limited to my students. There's a common cultural myth that informational texts are inherently boring—albeit practical and necessary to know. And yet, watch what people share online. They aren't sending stories and novels back and forth. They're sharing high-interest articles. It isn't necessarily practical, either. Often, what they share online are informational texts that pique their natural curiosity.

I want my students to have the same sense of joy and wonder about informational texts. I want them to ask questions and find fascinating facts about their world. This is why we have Wonder Days in our class. The idea here is for students to go from inquiry to research to creativity in a few class periods. I have had success in arranging students in small groups or pairs. However, it tends to work best with students working alone.

We start with the concept of wonder. Students use the sentence stem of "I wonder why _____," or "I wonder how _____," or even "I wonder if _____." I explain that the parameters have to be fact-based. In other words, "I wonder why jellyfish don't sting themselves" works perfectly but "I wonder why there is suffering in the world" doesn't quite fit this mini-project.

Afterward, students create questions that are fact-based and connected to their wonder statements. Typically, students type their questions into a Google Document. However, it has also worked to use a research table in the form of a spreadsheet. Afterward, we walk through the research process:

- Step One: Create their questions (if they finished Part One, you're good)

- Step Two: Search by using the right keywords
- Step Three: Identify the source based upon text complexity
  - Can I read this text?
  - Can I pick apart the meaning of the words using vocabulary strategies?
  - Are there any verb tenses that I don't understand? If so, is there a verb tense formula I can use to decode it?
- Step Four: Analyze the bias of the source
  - Is this source true?
  - Is this source accurate?
  - Is there any bias in this source?
- Step Five: Analyze the information
  - Is this information accurate? Could this be verified by other sources?
  - Is there any bias that should concern me?
  - Does this answer my question?
- Step Six: Paraphrase the information
  - Put this into their own words right under the question
  - Use sentence stems if necessary
- Make sure to cite their sources

Students can select which tools work best for each part of the research process. For example, some students might prefer keeping a tab open with the website while others might copy and paste the website text into a shared document where they annotate it for facts, bias, and language. Some students might paraphrase into a document while others prefer a spreadsheet (with a research grid) or a digital index cards. The key here is that every child feels empowered to choose which tools work best for which tasks.

Students may find fascinating facts that aren't connected to their questions. If that's the case, they can add a question and an answer. The fun part of research is that they never know what fascinating facts are going to pop out at you. As a teacher, there may be some parts that are too confusing for some students. Here's where one-on-one conferencing or small group research instruction can be helpful.

After they have their questions and their answers finished, they get to choose how they want to display their answers. The first is a Q+A blog post with the questions and the answers. As an extension, students can take the facts and create a "Seven Things You Might Not Know About _____" blog post.

Some students might want to do a podcast. Here, they partner up with a classmate and do a Q+A expert interview about the research. The first part should be a short introduction. The second part should be an interview of partner A to B. Afterward, they can switch and then end with a conclusion. Teachers can integrate this culminating activity into a weekly or monthly podcast, where students get the chance to improve in their oral language development as they increase in their comprehension of informational texts.

Another option is a slideshow where they show five fascinating facts they learned alongside five Creative Commons photographs. This inclusion of visual material helps solidify vocabulary.

As students move through the entire research process, they get a chance to focus on the facts they are learning rather than focusing on completing a task. With a higher level of engagement and a deeper sense of motivation, they often take bigger risks and tackle tougher texts. However, because the teacher has added layers of scaffolding, the task remains at a challenging level without being so challenging that students give up.

DIGITAL LITERARY CIRCLES AND DISCUSSION GROUPS

Digital tools also allow students to connect with a global audience. One example is a global literary circle. Here, students use a social network to engage in meaningful conversations around the themes of a specific work. Unlike a face-to-face literary circle, the asynchronous and long-distance elements allow ELL students to take their time in crafting responses. The instant access to tutorials and sentence stems allow students to engage in meaningful dialogue without feeling left behind by native speakers.

A teacher might want to begin the literary circles by creating specific questions, along with optional sentence stems that students can use. Over time, the students can begin crafting their own questions by using flexible question stems. Eventually, they grow less dependent on the scaffolding as they craft questions and answers in the ongoing global conversations around a literary work.

It doesn't have to be limited to fellow readers. With the sheer number of digital tools, students are now able to connect with authors in ways never seen before. Author Skypes, Google Hangouts (recorded or live), and Twitter chats allow students long-distance access to authors who might not typically have a chance to visit the school. Teachers can provide sample questions, sentence stems, and vocabulary strategies to help ELL students prepare for these conversations.

Online discussions do not need to be limited to literary circles. Sometimes the most authentic form of discussion occurs when students post articles, along with questions and thoughts, to a social network. Teachers can create larger, multiple-class discussion spaces using a learning management systems. Other times, students can use tools like Voxer or Slack to discuss a particular article or topic using text, voice, and pictures. Each student can read a separate article and cite different facts in an ongoing discussion about a central theme, question, or topic. This allows students of varying language levels to participate in rich discourse while still reading texts at their independent reading levels.

MOBILE FLUENCY

Digital tools can take some of the traditional reading activities to a whole new level. Consider reading fluency. Traditionally, a student reads a particular text aloud and measures how many words he or she can read in a given amount of time. However, with a mobile device, students can now assess their own progress.

Students begin by pressing record on their device and reading the passage. Using the stopwatch app, they can set a timer as they press record. I found that it works best to have one student reading/recording while a second partner checks for mistakes and keeps time. It also works well to have students go outside, away from the noise of the classroom. Afterward, the students switch roles of reading and keeping track of mistakes.

Next, students access an online form (Google Forms work well) and listen to their own read aloud. The online form works as a self-assessment rubric allowing students to fill out the fluency data (words and mistakes) while also rating themselves in pace, accuracy, and expression. Students often point out things that they had missed before (such as tone or mispronunciation). While the process might be simple, the results can be profound as students analyze their own reading process and make goals for self-improvement.

FINAL THOUGHTS

Differentiated reading can be a real challenge, especially when teachers want to match the standards with student interests. It's even more challenging when there are language issues that students must navigate. However, digital tools offer choice and differentiation in content while also empowering students through social connections.

Next Steps

- Develop sentence stems for reading discourse. The more students wrestle with the text using academic language, the more they will improve as readers.
- Take an interest inventory on the first week of school. Use this to help find high-interest informational reading.

●●● FOR REFLECTION ●●●

1. There is often an antitechnology bent among literacy and reading teachers. How do you combat this mindset?

2. How do you keep kids interested in reading and free from distractions while they are doing digital reading?

3. Why do so many people believe that informational text is "necessary but boring"? How can you combat this cultural misconception?

4. What are some strategies for personalizing reading?

Conclusion

Developing a Framework

A group of visitors walked into my classroom toward the end of the year. At one table, students were debating an idea on a podcast. At another table, students were working on the finishing touches of their Create a Product project. Meanwhile, a few solitary students tapped away on their laptops, crafting their ideas on their blogs.

On the surface, it looked messy. It looked like an unstructured free-for-all that had somehow led to a high level of engagement.

A visitor commented, "I like how you have managed to leave them alone and let them choose their own learning."

However, that's not how it worked at all. This beautiful, chaotic, personalized moment wasn't the end result of a free-for-all. Instead, it was product of a full year of highly structured learning opportunities. The sentence stems, tutorials, verb tense studies, and vocabulary blogs were all part of a series of structures that students were continuing to access in order to engage with the language.

PARADIGM SHIFTS

It looks loose and unstructured because the structures rarely get in the way. The scaffolding works as a bridge rather than a barrier and, even though I fail at times, I try to stick to a philosophy of providing just enough language support to allow students to be as free as possible. This only works because students act as self-directed thinkers, empowered to make decisions about their own learning. The following are some paradigm shifts that have allowed this to work in my classroom:

- *From Teacher Choice to Student Choice:* Initially, I attempted to find the best high-interest reading I could for students. I spent the summer coming up with projects that I thought they would enjoy. However, over the course of a semester, I realized that students should be part of the project-planning phase. I embraced student inquiry and incorporated Genius Hour into our daily schedule.

- *From Teacher Monitoring to Student Monitoring:* By implementing student-teacher conferencing and offering student progressing monitoring tools, students were empowered to monitor their own progress and set their own goals in language acquisition. Students used asynchronous conferencing and digital productivity tools to track their own progress and grow in their metacognition.

- *From Rigid Processes to Flexible Strategies*: The first time my students engaged in vocabulary annotation, I taught them a rigid system with different highlight colors representing different ideas. I had a six-step process on a poster and I expected students to follow it. Unfortunately, they focused so much on the rigid process that they missed the meaning of vocabulary. Over time, we shifted to viewing strategies as flexible, allowing students to customize each approach to fit their own needs.

- *From Isolated Assignments to Project-Based Learning:* By using a project-based learning framework, my students spent less time completing individual assignments and more time seeing the connections between ideas. Larger themes emerged as they tackled bigger questions. Students felt empowered to make something that mattered to them. So, while the language acquisition piece remained highly structured, the project-based learning framework allowed them to move through things at their own pace with a higher level of ownership.

- *From Creativity as Enrichment to Creativity as a Daily Essential*: Digital tools empower students to make things. It could be a blog post, a design project, a podcast, a website, a documentary, or a coding project. Here creativity wasn't relegated to an extension activity for those who had earned enrichment. Instead, it was a daily, integral part of the routine.

WHAT THIS LOOKS LIKE: DESIGN PROJECTS

During our unit on probability, students worked on creating the ultimate board game. We used the same design thinking cycle that students had used throughout the year. It began with understanding the audience (the empathy phase) and thinking through a problem (in this case, a need for entertainment and amusement). Next, they moved into the research phase. Here, they conducted both market research and historical research on board games. They developed their own essential questions such as "What makes a board game addicting?" or "Why would a board game become popular?" Looking back on it, students could have reached out to the connected community to interview both fans and designers in the board game industry.

Next, students moved into the ideation phase and eventually set up a plan. From there, they built and tested prototypes. For days, they worked on refining their prototypes by testing the games out with fellow classmates and using surveys to improve the design. Finally, students finished their product and moved into the marketing phase. Here, each group created an audio and video advertisement along with a website.

This design process wasn't new to students. We had used the same process in studying causes, effects, and solutions to social issues. We had used the cycle when students created blogs and documentaries. So, the design thinking framework felt like a normal progression to students. Similarly, students were already used to creating essential questions, conducting researching, and making models.

Students analyzed the elements of probability and experimentation that they were learning in math. They wrote expository, functional, and persuasive texts based upon what they had learned in language arts. I added checklists asking students to practice difficult grammatical structures and students practiced oral language development through the discourse stems students used during the breaks in the project.

The end result was something creative, connecting concepts from every discipline into one larger project. It was highly structured but it never felt that way. Instead, it felt flexible and fun.

THE POWER OF DIGITAL PLATFORMS

Digital platforms allow users to be more connective and creative with media. Sadly, many ELL students never get the opportunity to use digital tools in a creative and connective way. However, with the integration of quality language acquisition strategies, teachers can provide the bridges that allow students to access information, develop concepts, craft their own work, and share their voice with a global audience. At that point, digital platforms become truly transformational—but only as a result of the real transformation that occurs as a result of great teaching. Tools are amazing but they are nowhere near as amazing as the teachers who tirelessly work to create opportunities where students gain the ability and the confidence to find their voice.

CORWIN A SAGE Company

CORWIN HAS ONE MISSION: to enhance education through intentional professional learning.

We build long-term relationships with our authors, educators, clients, and associations who partner with us to develop and continuously improve the best evidence-based practices that establish and support lifelong learning.

Solutions you want. Experts you trust. Results you need.